**WITHDRAWN
AND
DONATED
FOR SALE**

Hello, Family Members,

Learning to read is one of the most important accomplishments of early childhood. **Hello Reader!** books are designed to help children become skilled readers who like to read. Beginning readers learn to read by remembering frequently used words like "the," "is," and "and"; by using phonics skills to decode new words; and by interpreting picture and text clues. These books provide both the stories children enjoy and the structure they need to read fluently and independently. Here are suggestions for helping your child *before*, *during*, and *after* reading:

Before
- Look at the cover and pictures and have your child predict what the story is about.
- Read the story to your child.
- Encourage your child to chime in with familiar words and phrases.
- Echo read with your child by reading a line first and having your child read it after you do.

During
- Have your child think about a word he or she does not recognize right away. Provide hints such as "Let's see if we know the sounds" and "Have we read other words like this one?"
- Encourage your child to use phonics skills to sound out new words.
- Provide the word for your child when more assistance is needed so that he or she does not struggle and the experience of reading with you is a positive one.
- Encourage your child to have fun by reading with a lot of expression...like an actor!

After
- Have your child keep lists of interesting and favorite words.
- Encourage your child to read the books over and over again. Have him or her read to brothers, sisters, grandparents, and even teddy bears. Repeated readings develop confidence in young readers.
- Talk about the stories. Ask and answer questions. Share ideas about the funniest and most interesting characters and events in the stories.

I do hope that you and your child enjoy this book.

—Francie Alexander
Reading Specialist,
Scholastic's Learning Ventures

PHOTO CREDITS

pages 4 National Portrait Gallery, Smithsonian Institution

pages 9, 22, 32 Schomburg Center for Research in Black Culture, New York Public Library

page 11 top: The Historical Society of Pennsylvania: "African Episcopal Church of St. Thomas in Philadelphia, A Sunday Morning View." Lithograph by William Breton, [Accession #Bb862B756#44]; bottom: Absalom Jones, [Leon Gardiner Collection Box 7Gf.1]

pages 12, 18, 20, 21, 29, 31, 38, 39, 42, 43, 46 Corbis

page 15 Collection of the New-York Historical Society

pages 27, 37 Library of Congress

page 40 AP/Wide World

Produced by Just Us Books, Inc.
356 Glenwood Avenue
East Orange, NJ 07017

No part of this publication may be reproduced, or stored in a retrieval system, or transmitted in any form or by any means, electronic, mechanical, photocopying, recording, or otherwise, without written permission of the publisher. For information regarding permission, write to Scholastic Inc., Attention: Permissions Department, 555 Broadway, New York, NY 10012.

Text copyright © 2001 by Wade Hudson.
Illustrations copyright © 2001 by Ron Garnett.
All rights reserved. Published by Scholastic Inc.
SCHOLASTIC, HELLO READER, CARTWHEEL BOOKS and associated logos
are trademarks and/or registered trademarks of Scholastic Inc.

Library of Congress Cataloging-in-Publication Data
Hudson, Wade.
  Great Black heroes: five bold freedom fighters/by Wade Hudson; illustrated by Ron Garnett.
      p. cm.   — (Hello reader! Level 4)
           ISBN 0-590-48026-X
  1. Afro-American civil rights workers—Biography—Juvenile literature. 2. Afro-American political activists—Biography—Juvenile literature. 3. Heroes—United States—Biography—Juvenile literature. 4. Afro-Americans—Civil rights—History—Juvenile literature. [1.Afro-Americans—Biography. 2. Civil rights workers. 3. Political activists.] I. Garnett, Ron, ill. II. Title. III. Series.
                              E185.96.H775 2001
323'.092'396073—dc21   00-041003

12 11 10 9 8 7 6 5 4 3   03 04 05
                    Printed in the U.S.A.   23
                    First printing, February 2001

GREAT BLACK HEROES

Five Bold Freedom Fighters

by Wade Hudson

Illustrations by Ron Garnett

Hello Reader! — Level 4

Scholastic Inc.

New York   Toronto   London   Auckland   Sydney
Mexico City   New Delhi   Hong Kong

Produced by Just Us Books, Inc.

Richard Allen
BORN 1760 - DIED 1831

First National Black Leader

It was a November day in 1787 in the city of Philadelphia, Pennsylvania. Richard Allen and several of his friends entered St. George's Methodist Episcopal Church to attend services. The group headed for the seats that had been set aside for Blacks. Right away a *sexton*, a church officer, pointed them upstairs to an area called the gallery. Richard and his friends thought the order was strange. They had always been allowed to sit downstairs in special chairs along the walls of the sanctuary. Now they were being directed upstairs. However, no one protested. They simply obeyed.

As the group walked to the gallery, a church leader began to pray. Richard and his friends stopped and kneeled.

"You must get up! You must not kneel here!" the sexton said. He tried to pull Absalom Jones, a member of the group, to his feet.

"Wait until the prayer is over," Absalom whispered.

"No, you must get up now!" the sexton insisted.

"Wait until prayer is over and I will get up and trouble you no more."

The angry sexton beckoned for other church members to assist him, but the prayer soon ended. Richard, Absalom Jones, and the others walked out of St. George's Church and never returned. Their response is believed to have been one of the first protests by free Blacks in America. A few years later, Richard Allen would establish one of the first churches for Blacks. And he

Richard Allen and Absalom Jones kneel in prayer while a church sexton yells for them to move.

would earn the title, "Father of the Black Church."

Richard was born into slavery in 1760 in Philadelphia. When he was still a little boy, he and his family were sold to a man who owned a plantation in Dover, Delaware. It was rare for an entire family to be sold together. Richard felt fortunate, because he loved his family very much. A short while later, however, Richard's good fortune changed. His mother, father, and three of his brothers and sisters were sold to another slave owner. This made young Richard very sad. He became extremely depressed. He couldn't understand why his people had to suffer so much under the cruel system of slavery. Richard turned to God for an answer.

In the safety of a nearby forest, Richard learned to read and he studied the Bible. By the time he reached his teenage years, he knew that for God there was neither Black nor White. God loved all his people equally. So Richard decided he was

Bethel African Methodist Episcopal Church was founded by Richard Allen.

going to dedicate himself to God and preach the word of God to others.

One day, Richard convinced his master to let him and his brother hire themselves out so they could earn money to buy their freedom. After buying his freedom, Richard traveled throughout Delaware, Pennsylvania, and Maryland, preaching to Blacks and Whites. Richard continued to study the Bible and other books as he traveled. Soon, he made his way back to the city of Philadelphia. In Philadelphia, Richard Allen would make some of the most important contributions to the cause of Black Americans.

In 1794, Richard established Bethel African Methodist Episcopal Church, one of the country's first Black churches. Thus he was called the "Father of the Black Church."

In 1816, he was chosen to be bishop of the African Methodist Episcopal Church, one of the first national church groups he helped to organize. Richard was also elected president of the first Black convention in 1830. The convention drew Black leaders from many states and was held to discuss ways to abolish slavery and end discrimination.

Some have also called Richard the country's "first national Black leader." Along with Absalom Jones, he organized the Free African Society, one of the first Black organizations established in the United States.

Richard Allen founded a day school for

Richard's friend Absalom Jones (below) founded the St. Thomas African Episcopal Church in Philadelphia.

Black children in Philadelphia and a night school for adults. This tireless fighter dedicated his life to the struggle of freedom for Blacks. He was 71 years old when he died in 1831.

Harriet Tubman
BORN CIRCA 1820 - DIED 1913

Moses of Her People

Harriet Tubman!

From 1850 to 1860, that name struck terror into the hearts of slave owners everywhere. Posters offering $40,000 for her capture could be found tacked on the walls of railroad stations and on trees throughout the South.

WANTED DEAD OR ALIVE!

That's what the posters read. Most slave owners would prefer that Harriet be delivered dead. But if she had to be captured alive, that would be all right, too. Just stop her! That's all they wanted.

No one had caused these slave owners more trouble than the small, determined Black woman some people called Moses. An escaped slave, she made trip after trip to the South to help other slaves escape to freedom in the North. She made these dangerous trips to and from the South between 1850 and 1860.

Bounty hunters couldn't catch her. Law officials couldn't stop her. She was brave, cool and cunning, and very smart. Harriet led more than 300 slaves to freedom. And she was proud that not one of them was ever captured.

Harriet Tubman was born around 1820 or 1821 in Bucktown, near Cambridge, Maryland. Like her ten brothers and sisters, her father, and her mother, she was a slave. By age five, Harriet was working full-time, cleaning the houses of White

Enslaved Blacks in the South worked long hours on plantations like this one in South Carolina.

families during the day and tending to their children at night.

Even as a young child, Harriet knew slavery was wrong. And as she grew older, she became more and more angry about the harsh treatment her people had to endure. When she reached her teenage years, her master grew tired of trying to make her a house servant. Harriet was sent to work in the field where she plowed, drove oxen, and did the same work the men had to do.

Harriet's hatred of slavery grew stronger and stronger. Once, she tried to stop an overseer on the plantation from attacking a fellow slave who had tried to run away. The overseer threw a two-pound weight at the escaping slave.

The weight struck Harriet instead, tearing a hole in her skull. She was only 13 years old.

The blow nearly killed young Harriet, but she eventually recovered. During her recovery, she developed a deep religious faith that she held on to for the remainder of her life.

Harriet continued life as a slave, even after she married John Tubman, a free Black. A slave was property, and a slave owner would never give up his property without being paid in return.

Harriet tried to stop an overseer from beating another slave. She was struck with a two-pound weight.

One day, Harriet heard that her master was going to sell her and two of her brothers to another slave owner. She decided she was going to run away. She tried to encourage her brothers to run away with her, but they were too afraid.

On a summer night in 1849, Harriet set out alone to reach freedom in the North. She was almost 30 years old. She traveled

Harriet and some of the people she helped to freedom.

at night through Maryland and Delaware until she reached Philadelphia and freedom. But Harriet was not satisfied with getting her own freedom. She was determined to free as many of her people as she could. For the next ten years, she devoted her life to leading slaves to freedom through the *Underground Railroad.* This was a secret group that helped runaways get to the North.

Abolitionist societies were organized groups that fought to end slavery. When members first heard about Harriet's great deeds, they invited her to speak at some of their meetings. Along with other freedom fighters, Sojourner Truth and Frederick Douglass, Harriet became a leading voice demanding the end of slavery.

In 1861 the war between the North and South began. It was called the Civil War. In the beginning, Blacks were not allowed to fight. So, Harriet volunteered her services as a nurse and as a spy. She, Frederick Douglass, and others continually

Harriet Tubman served as a nurse and a spy for the Union army.

urged President Abraham Lincoln to allow Blacks to fight in the war that could end slavery. Finally, in 1862, the President issued an order that permitted Blacks to enter the Union army. Thousands of Blacks joined. Harriet Tubman used the same determination and courage she showed on the Underground Railroad to lead Black troops into battle. The North won the war with important help from Blacks.

Harriet Tubman received many

Harriet Tubman Historical Home, Auburn, NY

honors during her life, including a medal from Queen Victoria of England. But this great freedom fighter spent her last years in poverty. The federal government refused to grant her monies she felt she had earned for her services to the Union Army during the Civil War. Finally, she was given the $20 a month her deceased husband had earned as a Union soldier. She used the money to help establish a place for the aged and needy in Auburn, New York.

Mary Church Terrell
BORN 1863 - DIED 1954

A Gentle Militant

Mary Church Terrell was born in 1863, the year the Emancipation Proclamation was issued. This law ended slavery in the South.

Compared to that of most Blacks during the late 1800s, Mary had an easy life. Her father Robert, a former slave, was one of the wealthiest men in the South. After first working hard on his White father's steamboat, Robert became a successful saloon keeper, banker, and real estate agent in Memphis, Tennessee. Mary's mother was a successful businessperson, too. She was a property owner and a dressmaker, and operated one of the most popular hair salons in Memphis. So Mary and her brother, Thomas, had the best their parents could offer. They lived a life of privilege.

Still, her father's money and his high position in the community could not protect them from the insults Blacks faced daily in America at that time.

Mary had her first encounter with racial discrimination while on a train trip with her father. A train conductor removed her from a seat reserved for Whites. Young Mary could not understand why she was forced from her seat. She knew she had done nothing wrong. Her father refused to talk about the incident, and he forbade her to talk about it, too. Mary, however, never forgot that incident.

With her family's wealth, Mary could have become a spoiled and pampered adult. She could have settled into an easy life at

While riding on a train with her father, Mary was forced by the conductor to move from a Whites-only section to an area assigned to Blacks.

home as her father wanted her to do. But Mary chose a different path. She chose to fight for equal rights for Blacks and for women.

From the time she was a little girl, Mary's parents wanted the best education possible for their daughter. When it came time for Mary to go to school, her mother and father didn't want her to attend the segregated schools in Memphis. Those schools did not offer Black students a quality education. So they sent her to a special primary school run by Antioch College in Yellow Springs, Ohio. Mary graduated from high school in Oberlin, Ohio. She then attended Oberlin College, one of the leading institutions of higher learning in the country. In 1884, she received a bachelor's degree.

"All during my college course, I had dreamed of the day when I could promote the welfare of my race," Mary once said.

Mary believed she could help her people by becoming a teacher. Her father

After Mary graduated from Oberlin College, her father wanted her to stay at home and take charge of the household.

didn't want her to teach. He wanted her to remain at home to take charge of his household and to entertain guests. After graduating from Oberlin College and spending several months at her father's home, Mary grew restless. She felt she was wasting her valuable education. So she applied for a number of teaching positions. She received an offer from Wilberforce University, the first American institution of higher learning for Blacks.

At Wilberforce, Mary did just about

everything. She taught reading, writing, mineralogy, and French. She served as secretary of the faculty, played the organ for Sunday services, and rehearsed the choir once a week. Mary remained at Wilberforce for two years

Next, Mary accepted a teaching position at the Preparatory School for Colored Youth in Washington, D.C. She taught in the foreign language department headed by Robert Terrell. Later, Mary went to Europe where she completed two years of study. Afterward, she returned to her teaching position in Washington, D.C. A year later she married Robert Terrell, who was now the principal.

One day, Mary received news from Memphis that Tom Moss, a childhood friend, had been hung by a lynch mob. Mary was crushed. She went to Frederick Douglass, a leader for Black causes. Mary and Frederick visited the White House to ask President Benjamin Harrison to condemn lynching. The President would not.

Mary Church Terrell was a founding member of the NAACP, which, on July 28, 1917, staged a silent protest parade on Fifth Avenue in New York City. The parade was in protest against violence to Blacks in America.

For the next 53 years, Mary Church Terrell fought to correct injustice and unfair treatment. She dedicated her life to the struggle for equal rights for Blacks and for women. In 1890, she was elected the first president of the National Organization for Colored Women, one of the first national organizations for Black women. She was a founding member of the National Association for the Advancement of Colored

People (NAACP), which was organized in 1909.

In 1920, the Nineteenth Amendment to the Constitution was passed, giving women the right to vote. It was the tireless efforts of women such as Susan B. Anthony, Elizabeth Cady Stanton, Carrie Chapman Catt, and Mary Church Terrell that won women this right.

Mary was a member of the District of Columbia Board of Education, the first Black woman in the country to be appointed to such a post. It was also through her efforts that a day was set aside to recognize Frederick Douglass, the great Black leader. Washington, D.C. schools were the first in the country to honor a Black person in this way.

In May 1954, the United States Supreme Court ruled that racial segregation, separation of the races, was unlawful. In July of that year, Mary Church Terrell died. This special lady had made a difference in the lives of so many.

Mary was a powerful public speaker and organizer. She made speeches at colleges and universities, and to organizations in the United States and in Europe.

Fannie Lou Hamer
BORN 1917 - DIED 1977

A Brave Civil Rights Leader

One day in 1962, a bus with 18 Black Americans seated inside pulled up to the courthouse in Indianola, Mississippi. Nervous and scared, these men and women were about to take one of the most important steps in their lives. They were going to go inside the courthouse and try to register to vote! In 1962, a Black person in Mississippi could lose his or her life for doing that.

One of the 18 people on the bus was a woman named Fannie Lou Hamer. On this day, her life would change. She would soon become an important leader in the struggle to end *segregation,* separation of Blacks from Whites, in the South.

As they looked out the windows of the bus, the men and women could see the police and state troopers gathered in front of the courthouse.

Would the group get up enough courage to walk past the police and enter the courthouse? No one moved. Suddenly, Fannie Lou got up and walked off the bus. She marched right past the police and into the courthouse. The other Blacks followed. They were forced to take a literacy test. These tests were used to help keep Blacks from voting. Everyone from the bus failed the test.

Soon after that day, Fannie Lou's life was threatened and she was kicked off the farm where she lived and worked. When she went to stay with a friend, 16 bullets were fired into the house. But that didn't

Fannie Lou tries to register to vote in her home state of Mississippi.

stop Fannie Lou. She went back three more times to take the literacy test.

In January 1963, she finally passed and became a registered voter. Then she began helping others prepare for the test. Fannie Lou was now a civil rights activist. She joined other civil rights activists and quickly became a leader in the struggle to change the unfair system in the South.

Fannie Lou was the last of 20 children born to Jim and Louella Townsend. When she was a child, she was stricken with polio, which left her with a limp. Fannie Lou began picking cotton when she was six years old. After she married, she worked as a sharecropper on the same farm where she had grown up.

Day after day she worked in the hot Mississippi sun. She and her husband had no children of their own, but Fannie Lou was a mother to the children of other parents. She was a respected member of her community. People looked up to her and came to her for advice and information. So it was no surprise that this brave woman

Sharecroppers worked long hours for a small share of the crop. They barely earned enough to support their families.

became a leader, risking her life time and time again.

Once, she and a few colleagues stopped to eat at a Whites-only restaurant in a bus terminal in Winona, Mississippi. Fannie Lou was beaten, arrested, and thrown in jail. While in jail, policemen ordered two Black prisoners to beat her until they were exhausted. She nearly lost sight in one eye, and one of her her kidneys was injured from the blows she received.

But Fannie Lou continued to fight. In 1964, she co-founded the Council of Federated Organizations. This organization recruited White students from the North to protest the treatment of Blacks in the South.

She helped set up the Mississippi Freedom Democratic Party to challenge the White-controlled Democratic party. The new party worked to gain equal representation in Mississippi politics.

Fannie Lou Hamer was a true champion for the civil rights of her people. Her most famous words capture the feelings of many Blacks during the 1960s. Explaining why she got involved in the civil rights movement, she said, "I'm sick and tired of being sick and tired!"

She died in 1977.

Above: Fannie Lou spoke at the Democratic Convention held in Chicago, Illinois, in 1968.
Left: TV newscaster John Chancellor, with glasses, watches police bar Fannie Lou Hamer and other members of the Mississippi Freedom Democratic Party (MFDP) who are trying to enter the convention hall in Atlantic City, New Jersey.

Medgar Wiley Evers
BORN 1925 - DIED 1963

A Warrior in the Struggle

It was nearing midnight. Medgar Evers was very tired as he drove toward his home in Jackson, Mississippi. Several affairs sponsored by the National Association for the Advancement of Colored People (NAACP) had lasted a little longer than he expected. Although he wanted to be home with his wife and children, he had to carry out his responsibilities as state field director of the NAACP.

Ten days before his death, Medgar Evers was arrested along with NAACP secretary Roy Wilkins for picketing a Woolworth's store in Jackson, Mississippi.

It was his job to recruit new members, encourage Black voter registration, and to investigate racial harassment and lynching.

It was a very difficult job. Some people considered Mississippi the most segregated state in the country. Medgar was a target for Whites who wanted their state to remain as it had been for many, many years. Just several weeks earlier, someone had tried to set Medgar's home on fire. The police had clubbed and arrested hundreds of Black high school students who were marching in support of the NAACP. The NAACP had organized sit-ins at a Woolworth store to protest segregation in Jackson.

This night, as soon as Medgar got out of his car, several shots rang out. Medgar fell to the ground. Fifty minutes later, the civil rights leader was dead. He was barely 38 years old.

The news of Medgar Evers' death

Charles Evers comforts his brother Medgar's children at funeral services for Medgar. Medgar's wife, Myrlie, is at right.

angered thousands of Americans, Black and White. Many of them wondered how much further some Whites would go to keep Blacks from obtaining their rights as citizens.

Byron De La Beckwith, a founding member of a White hate group in Mississippi, was eventually arrested for the murder of Medgar. There were two trials, but all-White juries refused to find De La Beckwith guilty.

Medgar Evers' death gave new courage to those fighting for the rights of Blacks in the South. More determined than ever, they vowed to continue the cause for which Medgar Evers had given his life.

Medgar Wiley Evers was born in Decatur, Mississippi, in 1925. He was the third of four children who lived with their father and mother on a small farm. Like other Black Mississippians at the time, the family faced discrimination and prejudice every day. When he was a boy, White kids threw rocks and yelled nasty things at

When Medgar was a young boy, Whites would taunt and throw rocks at him.

Medgar and his friends as they walked to school. When Medgar was 12 years old, a close friend of his family was lynched by angry Whites who said the friend had talked back to a White woman. That's the way life was for Blacks in Mississippi during that time.

Medgar joined the army after graduating from high school and fought in World War II. Two years after he returned home, he entered Alcorn A & M College where he

Public facilities were separated by race in the South.

majored in business administration. During his senior year, he married Myrlie Beasley, a fellow student. After graduating, Medgar and his family moved near his hometown, where he began a career as an insurance salesman.

One day, Medgar was in a hospital in Union, Mississippi, to visit his father who was sick. When he stepped outside to get a breath of fresh air, he saw a mob of angry Whites. A Black man had been injured during a fight with a White man and had been taken to the hospital by the police. The crowd had come to get him.

"I just stood there and everything was too much for me," Medgar said. "It was that way for my daddy, it was that way for me, and it looked as though it would be that way for my children. I was so mad I just stood there trembling and tears rolled down my cheeks."

Medgar quit his insurance job and went to work for the NAACP. Within two years, he was named state field director. In this job, Medgar fought to integrate public facilities, schools, and restaurants in Mississippi. He organized voter registration drives and demonstrations. He was an excellent spokesman for the rights of Blacks. His life was threatened many times by those who opposed granting Blacks their equal rights. But Medgar continued to press on until his death.

Following Medgar's funeral, more than 3,000 people from around the country marched behind the hearse bearing his body. Four days later, he was buried at Arlington Cemetery, a national cemetery reserved for those who have died in service to their country. Later in 1963, the NAACP awarded Medgar Evers its highest honor, the Spingarn Medal.

In 1994, after nearly thirty years, Byron De La Beckwith was finally convicted of murdering Medgar. Thanks to the efforts of people like Medgar Wiley Evers, Mississippi has come a long way.